D1109044

Discover your Soul Connection

Introducing LIVING IN ALIGNMENT

Darcy S. Clarke

Introduction by Wayne Marshall Jones

Acknowledgements

I **OFFER** gratitude to my Soul for teaching my human self how to live in alignment. At every step of the way my Soul has provided me with guidance in experiencing Soul realization and Soul actualization.

I offer gratitude to my late mother Jeannine for offering her abiding love, support, and encouragement to live authentically and for fostering my spirituality.

I offer gratitude to all the people who have served as my teachers over the years: Jacqueline Small, Caroline Myss, Gary Zukav, Pia Melody, Jack Kornfield, Fritz Perls, Ann Wilson Schaef, Alan Seale, Eckhart Tolle, and many others.

I offer gratitude to my friends and family members for their ongoing support and encouragement.

I offer gratitude to my colleague Wayne Marshall Jones for writing the first chapter of this book as well as his coaching, consultation, editing, proofreading, and book/cover design. His steadfast dedication and attention to detail are invaluable. His knowledge and skill base have been instrumental in bringing forth the Living in Alignment body of work.

I offer gratitude to my beloved cat Bodhi, who has been the mascot for this project. His love and affection have helped sustain me for the duration of this endeavor.

I offer gratitude to all the people I have worked with over the years; those who have placed their trust in me to serve as a catalyst for their healing and transformative processes. They have been my teachers, and their lives have been laboratories in assisting me to develop this material into its current manifestation.

To all of you I express my heartfelt appreciation.

Many blessings,

Darcy S. Clarke, MA LPCC CADAC-II CTPC

Contents

Preface

YOUR birthright is to *discover your Soul connection.* Your chosen path of Living in Alignment with your Soul will unfold organically. You do not have to adopt anyone's *belief system* or accept any dogma.

Living in Alignment is a self-directed process of *personal transformation.* You do not need a go-between or intermediary to access your Soul's wisdom and begin Living in Alignment.

To connect with your Soul, the only requirement is that you be *receptive:* opening your *heart* and mind with the intention of tuning into your Soul's messages. Only you can make this choice!

Living in Alignment is about developing a *partnership* between your human self and your Soul. To deepen your Soul connection, you will need all the intuitive skills you've developed in other relationships.

Although your mind can be distracted by *societal conditioning* and external influences, no one and nothing can interfere with your Soul connection unless you allow it. The deepening of your Soul connection will depend on how consciously open and receptive your mind is *willing* and your heart is *longing* to be.

The Living in Alignment Program is intended to assist you to create optimal conditions to *thrive* in your life and *experience Soul fulfillment.* This individualized interactive learning process offers you both a working understanding of the main concepts of Living in Alignment and an effective, practical skill base to *partner with your Soul* and begin Living in Alignment.

Chapter 1

Introduction

by Wayne Marshall Jones

The Dilemma of Self-awareness

BECOMING increasingly aware of your unique human self and how you choose to relate to other people and the rest of the world around you can offer you 'the wisdom of no escape.'

At some point on your journey of awareness you can no longer retreat into satiated numbness, temporary distractions, or diminished self-awareness. At this moment of burning intensity and great curiosity, there is only one question resonating in your mind:

'What shall I do with the rest of my life?'

The intensity and promise of this moment can feel strangely exhilarating. It's as though an unseen door in your life suddenly opens to offer a glimpse of new possibilities and perhaps a hint of unimagined freedom.

And so we look within our cultural frame of reference for answers (if not *the* answer) to the eternal question posed by our self-awareness.

But wait a second! Would you let some other person or external authority dictate the answer to this question? Probably not. So let's look at the common cultural values that may have influenced your life choices until now.

IT *is one of the commonest of our mistakes to consider that the limit of our power of perception is also the limit of all there is to perceive.*
Charles Webster Leadbeater

What Our Culture Values

Achieving an optimal 'quality of life' in our culture is defined by material values that we absorb unconsciously. Mass advertising focuses on eternal youth, fabulous beauty, perfect bodies, great wealth, and unlimited leisure and sexual pleasure in an earthly paradise and ideal society filled with charming, brilliant, highly cultured people who look like us, speak our language, and use the latest technology.

We want others to offer us amazing food, clothe and shelter us in great luxury, look after our best interests, and give us every opportunity for innovative education, personal development, advanced transportation, and global travel that we can imagine.

We want to be free from the ravages of disease, poverty, war, overpopulation, cultural and political conflict, limited resources, air and water pollution, radioactive leaks, global warming, aging, disabilities, parasites, garbage dumps, space junk, and species extinction. We want others to solve these problems for us.

Some day scientists may be able to predict, control, limit, or prevent natural disasters: earthquakes, floods, tornadoes, hurricanes, tsunamis, volcanic eruptions, and meteor impacts. (Not to mention inventing new weapons to defend us against alien invaders!)

Should we wish to be more than the ultimate consumers, we want unlimited opportunities to contribute our unique talents and insights to the co-evolution of our planet in the universe. Or perhaps to have perfect children who would grow up with even more privilege and comfort than we have attained.

These deeply rooted cultural values define in secular language our ultimate longings as human beings. We have created a system of rewards and punishments designed to promise us the ultimate satisfactions life has to offer if we can afford to pay for them and to deny us if we can't.

We realize that we have been driven primarily by these 'external resources' we've been promised. Yet intuitively we sense how *false and limiting* these desirable goods, services, and living environments are.

That's because we really want more than all that. There is something within each of us that yearns to participate in a more meaningful and deeply fulfilling experience of *who we really are* in an enriching community of others who feel the same way.

W HEN *we are unable to find tranquility within ourselves, it is useless to seek it elsewhere.*
François La Rochefoucauld

Improving Your Personal Quality of Life

Almost everyone is aware of his or her 'quality of life' issues. Whatever specifics you can name from your personal list, the *messy circumstances* of living can seem overwhelming. But there is a single key element that can be changed for the better: how you can focus your skills, energy, and intentions to create achievable breakthroughs that *transform* your personal quality of life.

If anyone has ever promised you that your personal transformation would be quick and easy to accomplish, guess what? They're flat wrong.

Sometimes the circumstances of your life simply can't be changed. Period. If this is the case, you know it. But what can be radically different is *how you decide to relate* to those life circumstances. Thus *who you are* in the circumstances life has given you can change radically.

The Experience of Living in Alignment

If you're focused primarily on being 'externally resourced,' Living in Alignment with your Soul is about experiencing another way to live your life. It's about discovering *a way of being your being* that is life-giving and life-sustaining because you are simply and profoundly being *your true self.*

8

Living in Alignment is about finding the 'freedom to be' *fully* your self. Living in Alignment frees you to focus solely on the one thing your life is really about and direct your whole life to calling into being that reality.

From the perspective of Living in Alignment you are actually co-creating your 'lived reality' from moment to moment. You can increase your *awareness* of how your mind is facilitating or hindering this process.

Living in Alignment is about developing a state of mind and a way of living that is *internally resourced* and *not* determined by what is or is not happening in your external world.

The *internal quality of life* you can begin to embody focuses on:

1. experiencing inspired living and an attitude of gratitude;

2. developing an increasing sense of joy, abundance, happiness, spontaneity, playfulness, and fun;

3. being present with yourself and others in your daily life;

4. knowing that you are deeply loved and not alone in your life;

5. finding a renewed sense of meaning and purpose in each chapter of your life;

6. opening your mind and heart to that which is beyond your human self;

7. discovering that your life is unfolding in ways that provide for all of your needs;

8. nurturing deeply satisfying relationships;

9. embracing your humanity and that of others;

10. being aware of and in the process of completing your life purpose;

11. realizing that you are benefitting from all of the experiences, conditions, events, and issues in your life.

> **I**MAGINE *you are a Masterpiece unfolding, every second of every day, a work of art taking form with every breath.*
> Thomas Crum

What if . . .

❖ you are more powerful and present than you ever imagined?

❖ you could tap the wisdom of the deepest part of yourself that you are unaware of?

❖ you could experience a profound connection with yourself, with other people, and with all of creation?

❖ you could discover your life purpose and your Soul mission?

❖ you are entirely 'free to be' your unique self?

And what if you discovered that all this about you is really true?

One way to experience this reality

This book is about the process of *discovering* these things about yourself. It's about how you can connect with your Soul—that deep, inner part of yourself that speaks to you even when you are not listening, when you are distracted, or when you're feeling upset or defiant. It's the still, small voice that whispers to you that there's more to you and the meaning of your life than you ever suspected. It's the voice of your longing for more life, more zest, and more fulfillment in this lifetime, not in some heavenly afterlife.

'But I'm skeptical!'

You can actually *tune into* the voice of your Soul entirely by yourself. You can learn to trust this part of yourself. You can stop getting in your own way and stop sabotaging your good intentions and best interests. You can even stop hating yourself for all you have done (or left undone) that has blocked your spiritual development.

The good news is that this book can help you get there. It's designed as a simple, concise, and understandable introduction to the process of Living in Alignment, a practical approach to personal transformation that you can pursue at your own pace and in your own way.

There are resources beyond this book to help you on your way. *Experience Living in Alignment,* the comprehensive guide, is for those who are ready to explore a program of self-development that could happen over a year (or less time for those ready to go faster). Certified LIA facilitators are trained to help you explore this path in greater depth as you deal with personal issues that may get in your way. Both group workshops and individual consultations with LIA facilitators are available to you.

This process was designed entirely with you in mind. There is **no hidden agenda** and no affiliation with any organization, cause, ideology, or belief system. It's all just for you and depends entirely on what you decide to do with it. You can design your own personalized version of Living in Alignment and take it where you want to go.

M AN *must first find his own soul.*
He who has found and knows his soul
   has found all the worlds,
   has achieved all his desires.
The Upanishads

'But do I *really* have a Soul?'

You don't have to buy into this 'Soul' business *or* this language, but I invite you to **explore** your own emerging awareness of your Soul (or whatever you want to call it). Using this approach to Living in Alignment, you'll be able to test out for yourself whether this reality is **true for you** and begin making your own life choices with your Soul's guidance.

Experiencing Your Soul

Like the wind that cannot be seen or contained but can be felt, you can sense your Soul by the *effects* of its presence and its workings in your daily life.

Your Soul expresses itself through qualities that are familiar to you. By bringing certain qualities to mind you can sense what your Soul is like.

The qualities that point to your Soul's reality are infinite. Here is a partial list. ☑ Check those that you experience in yourself and enjoy in others:

☐ Aliveness	☐ Faith	☐ Power
☐ Autonomy	☐ Freedom	☐ Presence
☐ Awe	☐ Fullness	☐ Serenity
☐ Beauty	☐ Generosity	☐ Spaciousness
☐ Certainty	☐ Goodness	☐ Stillness
☐ Clarity	☐ Grace	☐ Strength
☐ Compassion	☐ Gratitude	☐ Tenderness
☐ Contentment	☐ Innocence	☐ Truth
☐ Conviction	☐ Intelligence	☐ Unity
☐ Courage	☐ Joy	☐ Value
☐ Devotion	☐ Love	☐ Vitality
☐ Discernment	☐ Loyalty	☐ Wholeness
☐ Equanimity	☐ Openness	☐ Wisdom
	☐ Peace	

Everyone is capable of experiencing and expressing these qualities.

In each person certain qualities will be more apparent than others, and there are generally some that are more prominent than others.

Learning to recognize the qualities unique to your own Soul can help you identify them in others.

EXPRESSING *gratitude to the soul...*
creates a connection to the higher
dimensions of consciousness.
Richard Barrett

Try an Experiential Exercise

1. From the list on page 13 choose *one* of the qualities of your Soul that you'd like to explore and experience more of. This could be a quality you don't often experience fully.

2. Sitting or lying down comfortably in a quiet place, close your eyes when you're ready and breathe in and out slowly and consciously, letting go of whatever mental activity you notice.

3. As you breathe, let your mind focus on this quality and say the word aloud or to yourself with each slow in-breath.

4. Focus on what you experience when you imagine 'taking in' that quality with your in-

breath, holding your breath, and then releasing that quality into your surroundings with your out-breath.

5. Notice how quiet you feel inside as well as outside. If you notice any noises in your environment, just let them be for now. You may respond later if you wish.

6. Continue to breathe in and out for a few minutes until you are satisfied with your experience and ready to move on.

7. Open your eyes very gently without focusing on a particular object and just notice what you're feeling *in the Now*. Stay with that experience for a moment, just continuing to breathe into it.

8. Name this experience if a name occurs to you now. If not, words may occur to you later.

9. When you're fully ready, it's now time to do something else in your life if it occurs to you.

10. If not, you could do the exercise again, using another quality from the chart or a variation on your experience. Enjoy!

To explore deeper levels of awareness, see *Experience Living in Alignment*, Chapter 8: Deepening Your Awareness.

THE *soul never gives you a task that you are not equipped to handle.*
Richard Barrett

Develop your Reflective Practice

What are you experiencing right now? Try drawing, sketching, or doodling your feelings, ideas, and thoughts on paper, in a notebook or journal, or in a digital format. It's important to get in the habit of keeping your reflections in a portable format that respects your privacy and allows you easy access.

Try not to censor, edit, or perfect anything you create. Just let it flow as it will (or won't). If you're feeling blocked, stifled, or 'empty', take a slow walk with yourself, listen to music, dance, or do something different until inspiration happens. Then, when they come to you, use your opportunities to discover and reflect on what's happening in the world within yourself.

Hint: be *gentle* with yourself. And curious about what *wants* to come forth from within. Remember, you're not at war with your insights or trying to wrestle them to the ground in a headlock. Don't scare them off. Just let them come to meet you. Be in a *receptive* mood, and you will be rewarded.

THE *forms of the soul's intervention
are always loving, although they may
involve what appear to be negative
and painful situations.*
Richard Barrett

'But I'm *SO* messed up!'

Oh yes! But you're not alone. We all carry the burden of many years of *societal conditioning* that skews our self-perception, our experience of the world, and even our responses to life. Unconsciously we have become primarily *externally resourced*.

Living in Alignment is a process designed to *free you* from the constraints of your societal conditioning and to facilitate a transition to becoming *internally resourced* and discovering your *Soul mission*.

'So what *is* Living in Alignment anyway?'

First, here's what it's **not**:

1. It's **not** a new religion or cult.
2. It's **not** a get-rich-quick scheme or Ponzi scheme.
3. It's **not** a multi-level marketing scheme.
4. It's **not** a belief system or ideology.
5. It's **not** a guru-based road to spiritual enlightenment.
6. It's **not** a political or social or intellectual movement.
7. It's **not** a self-generating publishing empire.
8. It's **not** a source of opinions or advice.
9. It's **not** an inspiring success story to be imitated.
10. It's **not** the ultimate spiritual vision quest.
11. It's **not** the ultimate spiritual authority.
12. It's **not** everybody's new way to live.

13. It's **not** the latest, greatest way to solve all your problems.

In a nutshell, here's what it means to be Living in Alignment:

Living in Alignment with your Soul is a very different way of being and living your life. You will experience a transformative process of change: from being primarily *externally resourced* to being *internally resourced*. Instead of allowing societal conditioning and dictates to override your inner knowing or truth, you will learn to *listen to and follow the guidance* and promptings from your Soul. Living in Alignment with your Soul will foster your self-empowerment and facilitate your personal transformation.

T**WO** *roads diverged in a wood, and I —*
I took the one less traveled by,
And that has made all the difference.
Robert Frost

Chapter 2

'Why is it so difficult to access my Soul?'

IT is your human self, and more specifically your *conditioning*, that prevents you from accessing your Soul. The Living in Alignment approach has been developed to assist you to experience your Soul's presence in your life and learn how to *partner* with your Soul (or Source energy within). The Living in Alignment approach will also assist you to become increasingly more conscious/*aware* of the presence of your Soul in your life.

By conditioning I refer to how beliefs, thought forms, attitudes, perceptions, expectations, feelings, behaviors, and intentions are influencing your *connection* with your Soul (or lack thereof).

WITH *ordinary consciousness you can't even begin to know what's happening.*
Saul Bellow

Regardless of whether or not you believe this to be true, you alone are *choosing* the type of relationship you're having with your Soul on a moment-by-moment basis. You may be totally *unaware* of this experience. As in all relationships, it is your responsibility to nurture your connection with your Soul. Whatever you put into *deepening* your relationship with your Soul will be reflected in the quality of your connection.

Living in a *fear-based reality* hinders or outright prevents nurturing your Soul connection, for when you live in fear, your energy frequency is lowered and your human self goes into sympathetic (fight or flight) mode. Living in fear is an indicator of being primarily externally resourced (*stuck* in your head), making it difficult to access your intuition or hear the *voice* of your Soul. The more externally focused you are (identified with your human self and the three-dimensional world) the more you tend to live in fear.

Fear plays out as your human self (or your mind) wanting a guarantee, needing instant gratification, having resistance, doubts, and confusion, attempting to control the outcome, futurizing, etc.

Y*OU cannot expect
the world to change
until you change yourself.*
Robert Muller

It is also important to develop your ability to move from a *literal* understanding of events, circumstances, and experiences of your life to discover their *symbolic* meaning.

Like the air you breathe, your Soul is always present. You have only to open up to the 'bigger picture' of how all of the experiences you're having in life are serving/benefiting you and are integral to accomplishing your *Soul mission* or calling in life.

Your human self *gets in the way* of deepening your connection with your Soul by being impatient, jumping to conclusions, making hasty assumptions, aborting a process (a form of abandoning yourself), fearing the unknown, second-guessing, confusion, doubt, apprehension, being attached to a particular outcome, comparing your life to other peoples' lives, having a limiting view of Trust and Surrender ('giving up' vs. a merging of energy), and/or wanting instant gratification.

From the perspective of Living in Alignment *everything* that has happened, is happening, or will happen to you has the *inherent potential* of serving you. Another way of saying this is that all of your experiences are *intended* to provide you with maximum benefit. Your task is to train your mind to identify the insights, gifts, and lessons being offered and to *integrate* these into your behaviors.

Trust and *Surrender* are two of the most important requirements for your egoic mind to grasp and develop. Without this skill set in place, it becomes very difficult for your mind to listen to and follow the guidance of your Soul. The more your human self (or your mind) is identified with the three-dimensional world, the more difficult it may be to Trust and Surrender. Instead you will rely on your egoic mind that wants to stay in the driver's seat and will tend to *control* the outcome. To Trust and Surrender, your ego must *relinquish the illusion* that it can control the creative flow of Source energy (consciousness) that pulsates within all life forms.

From the perspective of Living in Alignment, Trust and Surrender are not just important concepts. When truly integrated into your life, Trust and Surrender are intended to *transform* your way of being and living in the world.

Your ability to Trust and Surrender directly impacts the *type* of relationship you have with your Soul and the world of Mystery. While having an open mind and heart are necessary to access your Soul, Trust and Surrender are essential to *deepening* your connection with your Soul.

Trusting in and surrendering to your Soul (or Source energy within) is about changing your *point of reference*, allowing your mind to defer to your Soul for guidance.

The act of trusting in and surrendering to your Soul is always *advantageous* — with no exceptions. You will be able to test this out for yourself.

The interplay of opening your mind and your heart fosters the development of your *intuition*, which is the voice of your Soul (or Source energy within).

E VERY *event is neutral.*
You give the situations
in your life all the meaning
they have for you.
Richard Barrett

From the perspective of Living in Alignment, you are *intended* to go about living your life in partnership with your Soul. It is by listening to and following the *guidance* of your Soul that you develop a *partnership* with your Soul. This is a cooperative venture in which your human self becomes the *agent* of your Soul.

In contrast, when you are primarily externally resourced you are living in fear, resulting in *worrying*. Worrying lowers your energy frequency by demanding a lot of energy. Worrying is an indicator that you are *not trusting* in Source energy and not working in partnership with your Soul.

Your need to *control and manipulate* are indicators that your *ego* is getting in your way. Contrary to popular misconceptions, trusting in your Soul (or Source energy) is *not* about having blind faith, and surrendering is *not* about becoming powerless. Trust involves *yielding* to your Soul, and Surrender involves *merging* with your Soul. The practice of trusting and surrendering translates to listening to and following the *guidance* from your Soul.

EXPECT *the best:*
convert problems into opportunities;
be dissatisfied with the status quo;
focus on where you want to go,
instead of where you're coming from;
and most importantly, decide to be happy,
knowing it's an attitude,
a habit gained from daily practice,
and not a result or payoff.
Denis Waitley

Chapter 3

Darcy's Story

A T the ripe old age of eight I knew that my Soul mission would be to 'help people find God in their lives' (hereafter 'a relationship with Source energy'). This was the response I received to the question I posed to Source energy about wanting to know my vocation in life.

If you haven't guessed already, I was a practicing Catholic at the time. Receiving this news offered my mind instant relief, for hearing this response felt 'right' through and through. Even though the nuns and priests at my school, along with my mother, would have rejoiced and been totally supportive upon hearing this news, I made the decision to keep this revelation to myself.

Being a practicing Catholic, I naturally thought that I would become a priest, and so I went about my business of being a kid, all the while pondering over this revelation. By age fifteen I realized that becoming a priest was *not* my calling in life after all. Even more surprising and somewhat shocking was being prompted by Source energy to leave the Catholic Church. For devout Catholics back then, even the *thought* of leaving the Church was considered sacrilegious. But *actually* leaving the Church! Well, that would be considered an outright abomination. Needless to say, I didn't consult the parish priest to gain his perspective about the guidance I received.

I was shaken up by this news, feeling both anxious and excited. At the time I recall thinking that my connection with Source energy was my *lifeline*, and that without this connection I wouldn't have a life worth living. In my uncertainty I made a *deal* with Source energy (another act Catholics considered blasphemous): that I would follow my prompting to leave the Church for one year, but that I would return to the Church if I felt at any time that my connection with Source energy was being undermined.

To my surprise, my absence *deepened* my connection with Source energy. I was both disturbed by the *unconventionality* of the guidance and intrigued about what the ramifications would be for my life. I was also left without a clue about the particulars of how I would assist people to find a relationship with Source energy in their lives.

So there I was at age sixteen, having made the decision to leave the Catholic Church, knowing that this decision represented a departure from the conditioning of organized religion and more specifically of the Church. *I was set free!* This was a pivotal turning point in my life. I was feeling energized as well as experiencing uncertainty about how I would go about accomplishing my vocation.

*L*IVED *to its full,*
life is not an external journey
in search of happiness,
but an internal journey
in search of meaning.
Richard Barrett

Now that I was set free from the shackles of organized religion, my life took on a renewed sense of meaning and purpose. I spent the next twenty years focused on individuating and differentiating: on becoming my own person.

This was a time of questioning the status quo; of identifying interests; of developing my processing skills; of taking a personal inventory; of addressing my shame, anger, fear, and emotional pain; of developing marketable skills and earning a living; of coming into a sense of my personal power; of reaching out and making new friends; of experimenting with drugs and altered states of consciousness; of exploring my sexuality; of reclaiming my power from people, events, and behaviors; of communing with nature and deepening my connection with the earth; of learning to live in my body; of leaving my family and my home state and traveling and living in various parts of the country; and of immersing myself in many different workshops and trainings.

In short, those twenty years were about *finding* myself, learning to *live authentically*, and *deprogramming* myself from unwanted, limiting societal conditioning. Throughout these twenty years I kept in the forefront the revelation that I was destined to 'assist people to find a relationship with Source energy in their lives.' Although I sensed that I was always *being guided*, I remained in the dark about the particulars of how I would actualize the revelation of 'assisting people to find a relationship with Source energy in their lives.'

The concern of not *knowing* how my life of service would unfold was no stranger to me, nor was *frustration* and *impatience* with the process. Despite my feelings of *doubt* and *insecurity* and the occasional *hissy fits*, my ability to Trust and Surrender to Source energy gradually continued to unfold.

T**HE** *route to personal happiness is not through serving self, but through serving others.*
Richard Barrett

As my processing skills developed and I gained more self-knowledge, I became increasingly aware that all the experiences, events, circumstances, positions, and situations in my life were of *significance*, and more specifically, that each was preparing me for *my calling* in life. This recognition offered me *solace* and kept me motivated to pursue my quest. It wasn't until my mid-thirties, however, that the information presented in the Living in Alignment body of work began making an indelible impression upon my mind.

W**HAT** *we are today comes from our thoughts of yesterday, and our present thoughts build our life of tomorrow. Our life is the creation of our mind.* The Buddha

Through a series of providential events it became perfectly clear to me that becoming internally resourced (listening to and following my Soul's guidance) was *a viable option* for living my life. This new understanding was affirmed by my Soul.

For a more detailed account, see *Experience Living in Alignment*, Chapter 1: Personal Introduction.

During this time I became aware that I was unknowingly allowing **societal dictates** to override my intuition about important life decisions and realized that this conflict had been going on for as long as I could remember.

Having acknowledged the poignancy of my predicament, I made the decision to pursue becoming internally resourced. Actually, I took this one step further by making a ***once-and-for-all*** decision to become internally resourced. And so for the next fifteen years I actively and wholeheartedly resolved to develop the skills necessary to become adept at listening to and following my Soul's guidance.

Shortly thereafter I had a lucid prophetic dream that affirmed for me that both **Soul realization** and

Soul actualization had become my reality. This dream also revealed that it would be of utmost importance for me to share with others what I've learned about the process of becoming internally resourced.

It would take another few years for me to recognize and acknowledge that teaching people to become internally resourced and to live in alignment was the means by which I would accomplish my Soul mission of 'assisting people to find a relationship with Source energy in their lives.'

O F *all the beautiful truths*
pertaining to the soul
which have been restored
and brought to light in this age,
none is more gladdening or
fruitful of divine promise and confidence
than this —
that man is the master of thought,
the moulder of character, and
the maker and shaper of condition,
environment, and destiny.
James Allen

Chapter 4

'Why Living in Alignment? Why Now?'

THE Living in Alignment body of work is a *response* to the world's ever-increasing 'madness'. In my opinion, this state of affairs represents an *imbalance* that is largely the result of people being disconnected from Source energy.

This 'madness' is seen in the random and organized cruelty, injustice, greed, corruption, needless suffering, wars, environmental destruction, egotism, abuse of power, misguided leadership, marginalization, discrimination, vast discrepancies in distribution of wealth, domestic violence, crime, homicides, mass starvation, and torture.

WE *cannot separate*
the healing of the individual
from the healing of the planet.
They are one and the same, because
the consciousness of each individual
is connected to the collective consciousness.
Although we are individuals,
we are also each part of the whole.
As we begin to heal ourselves as individuals,
we also naturally shift the consciousness
of the entire planet.
Shakti Gawain

This 'madness' is our *clue* that we are out of balance, and our cue to *realign* our human self with our Soul (the deepest aspect of who we are) as a means to *deepen* our connection with Source energy and live more consciously.

Going within to access your Soul's guidance will shed light on *how you can best respond* to the world's 'madness' (including your own). You will begin to understand how you are *intended* to foster *unity consciousness* in your own life and in the world around you.

This Introduction to Living in Alignment was written to inspire, entice, motivate, excite, encourage, and interest you in discovering or deepening your relationship with Source energy. My intention is to *illuminate* your life and the journey you're on.

Offering Living in Alignment is a *labor of love*, coming from a place of gratitude for the deepening, wondrous, and transformative connection with Source energy that the practice of Living in Alignment has offered me. It is also what I consider to be the *best gift* I could offer to the world.

> **T**HE *good life is to live on honorable terms with your own soul.*
> Saul Bellow

Chapter 5
'Is Living in Alignment for Me?'

ARE you ready to experience Living in Alignment?

☑ **Check the questions below that describe who you are and that are important to you.**

☐ Do you identify as agnostic?

☐ Do you identify as atheist?

☐ Have you lost your faith in a Power higher than yourself?

☐ Do you have anger or resentment toward Source energy?

☐ Do you feel neglected, betrayed, or abandoned by Source energy?

☐ Do you experience a lack of meaning or purpose in your life?

☐ Are you living in a fear- or shame-based reality?

☐ Do you have unresolved family-of-origin issues?

☐ Do you shrink from and/or despise people in positions of power and authority?

☐ Do you often get angry at your human self?

☐ Do you hold resentments toward yourself?

☐ Are you consumed with guilt or regrets?

☐ Are you feeling emotional pain?

☐ Are you feeling discouraged, hopeless, or helpless?

☐ Are you feeling despair or distress?

☐ Are you confused and doubtful about many things?

☐ Do you have existential inquiries?

☐ Are you living in 'victim consciousness'?

☐ Is it difficult to trust yourself or other people?

☐ Do you experience difficulty living authentically?

Are you interested in...

☐ fostering your own healing process?

☐ living up to your greatest potential?

☐ experiencing more joy, happiness, and fulfillment in your life?

☐ having relationships that are satisfying and life enhancing?

☐ finding a sense of meaning and purpose in your life?

☐ discovering your life calling/Soul mission?

Are you looking for a new perspective on your life when ...

☐ your thinking mind or personality is getting in your way?

☐ you are blocking yourself from achieving what you desire in life?

☐ you are experiencing being 'stuck'?

☐ you are feeling like you're at a dead end?

☐ you are no longer able to figure out your life (or something that is going on in your life) using your intellectual resources?

☐ you are feeling overwhelmed or confused?

☐ you have doubts about why you're here and living in a physical body?

☐ your relationships feel un-nurturing and draining?

☐ you are feeling caught up in your 'story' or that of others?

Do you want to...

☐ feel self-empowered?

☐ live up to your full potential?

☐ enjoy being in your physical body?

☐ engage fully in your life?

☐ contribute to the betterment of society?

Are you seeking to develop ...

☐ healthy self-esteem?

☐ deep, satisfying connections with others?

☐ a life that is abundant with joy, happiness, and fulfillment?

Along with answering **YES** to some or many of these questions, you'll have an intuitive sense that the Living in Alignment body of work will offer you some important information about yourself and the life you're living. Read on...

C URRENT *concepts of the mind-*
brain relation involve a direct break
with the long-established materialist
and behaviorist doctrine that had dominated
neuroscience for many decades. Instead of
renouncing or ignoring consciousness,
the new interpretation gives full recognition
to the primacy of inner conscious awareness
as a causal reality.
Roger W. Sperry

Chapter 6
The Living in Alignment Model

THE Living in Alignment body of work has one primary purpose: to assist you to **discover and experience** Source energy within yourself and in your life. In so doing you will find the direct link to realizing your true desires and creating a life that is filled with possibilities that are truly awesome, attainable, gratifying, and transformative!

YOU *are given the gift of the gods;*
you create your reality
according to your beliefs; yours is
the creative energy that makes your world;
there are no limitations to the self except
those you believe in.
Jane Roberts

The Living in Alignment approach is intended to:

❖ bridge the gap between science and spirituality

❖ foster your integrity

❖ facilitate your personal transformation

❖ offer concepts that expand your awareness

❖ assist you to live authentically

❖ facilitate your living up to your greatest potential

❖ illuminate the significance of your life

❖ deepen your connection with Source energy

❖ discover and actualize your Soul mission

❖ access Source energy directly

❖ illuminate how you are co-creating your life with Source energy

❖ keep your ego from getting in the way

❖ assist you to move out of fear- and shame-based realities

❖ foster unity consciousness

❖ facilitate grounding in the physical world

❖ assist you to appreciate and embrace your humanity

❖ assist you to reclaim your power from people, behaviors, conditions, and events etc.

Living in Alignment is intended as **a comprehensive** approach, either to augment and complement your existing resources or to help you design your own individualized spiritual practice.

The aim and distinguishing feature of the Living in Alignment Model is to foster a *partnership* between your human self and your Soul (or Source energy within).

The techniques utilized in the Living in Alignment process are derived from the author's personal experiences, many spiritual traditions, and various therapeutic modalities (such as Cognitive Behavioral, Transpersonal, Psychodynamic, Humanistic, Gestalt, Psycho-Spiritual, Solution-Focused, etc.).

WHEN *we align our thoughts, emotions, and actions with the highest part of ourselves, we are filled with enthusiasm, purpose, and meaning.*
Gary Zukav

The Living in Alignment approach will assist you to become more aware of the workings of Source energy in your life and to awaken you to the wonders of living in your human form.

The Living in Alignment perspective affirms that you are intended to *be your own expert* when it comes to knowing what your deepest needs, wants, and desires are and what will offer you meaning and purpose in your life.

Living in Alignment is a *lifelong practice* of becoming increasingly more present and aware of the experiences you are having, the significance of your life, and the roles you take on.

PAIN *and emotional discomfort have nothing to do with God's punishment. They are the result of an energy dynamic that reflects a lack of attunement of your personality with your soul.*
Richard Barrett

Living in Alignment is *a state of being* and living in the world that is in harmony with what is true in the Universe.

The Living in Alignment approach will increase your energy frequency. It will have a *synergistic* effect on your optimal functioning, yielding an overall sense of wellbeing and the most favorable results.

The information and skill base presented in the Living in Alignment body of work is designed to assist your human self in getting out of your way. In developing a partnership with your Soul, your mind is listening to and following your Soul's guidance and promptings. When this occurs, Living in Alignment becomes a reality, along with the experience of *discovering 'freedom to be' all of who you are*.

Living in Alignment moves you out of a *'me'* mentality to an *'us'* framework/perspective, illuminating the reality that everyone is *interconnected* and *interdependent*, and that your presence is intended to make a difference in people's lives — to truly be of service to others and vice versa.

The Living in Alignment approach is an *alternative way of being* and living your life that offers both short- and long-term benefits. These benefits are experienced whenever you listen to and follow the guidance/promptings from your Soul.

The Living in Alignment approach is for those who are yearning (or being called) to *wake up* in this lifetime; who are seeking to have a *conscious connection* with their Soul; who want to *deepen* this connection, *accelerate* their personal transformation, and/or acquire a language and context to *understand* what they have already begun to *experience*.

The Living in Alignment approach to living your life is *practical, effective,* and *trustworthy:*

❖ *practical:* Living in Alignment is user-friendly, attainable, and realistic.

❖ *effective:* Living in Alignment is well-founded, useful, powerful, sound, beneficial, and valuable.

❖ *trustworthy:* Living in Alignment is reliable, dependable, can be subjectively validated, and will stand the test of time.

O NLY *you can deprive yourself
of anything. Do not oppose
this realization, for it is truly
the beginning of the dawn of light.*
A Course in Miracles

O**NE** *has not only an ability*
to perceive the world,
but an ability to alter
his perception of it; or, more simply,
one can change things by the manner
in which one looks at them.
Tom Robbins

Chapter 7

Core Concepts of Living in Alignment

THE Core Concepts of the Living in Alignment Model are intentionally offered from a '*What if it is true?*' perspective.

I do not present the Core Concepts as a set of beliefs, nor do I advocate swapping one set of beliefs for another. Instead, you are encouraged to **question** and test out the validity of the Core Concepts for yourself in order to determine their practicality, effectiveness, and reliability.

The Core Concepts of the Living in Alignment Model are viewed as working hypotheses. I recommend that you allow yourself to have a subjective or **direct experience** of whatever it is that your mind is questioning.

MIND *is consciousness which has put on limitations.*
Sri Ramana Maharshi

Having an intellectual understanding of the Living in Alignment Core Concepts is important, and is usually necessary in order for your mind to take down its *defenses*. When your mental defenses are removed, you are ready to have direct experiences and be more available to track the *interplay* of these concepts in the co-creation of your life.

The more externally resourced you are, the more your mind will tend to require objective proof from outside authorities.

You are encouraged to substantiate the *validity* of the Living in Alignment Core Concepts by having direct *experiences* of them.

Y OU *will not grow if you sit*
in a beautiful flower garden,
but you will grow if you are sick,
if you are in pain, if you experience losses,
and if you do not put your head in the sand,
but take the pain and learn to accept it,
not as a curse or a punishment but as a gift
to you with a very, very specific purpose.
Elizabeth Kubler-Ross

The Living in Alignment approach will assist you to *examine* your conditioning (beliefs, perceptions, attitudes, expectations, behaviors) to determine which ones are *limiting* you or causing *unnecessary suffering* and getting in your way of thriving and living up to your greatest potential, along with offering a skill base to *modify* or *replace* unwanted conditioning.

The Living in Alignment approach will assist you to develop *a personal life philosophy* that is both life-affirming and congruent with universal principles (what is true in the universe).

YOUR *mind is a projector*
and your life is the screen.
Richard Barrett

Some of the Core Concepts of the Living in Alignment Model are listed below.

❖ Source energy is consciousness itself.

❖ We have a choice about the kind of relationship we have with Source energy.

❖ We can access Source energy directly and immediately.

❖ Our Soul is a unique aspect of Source energy within, while other people and life forms represent Source energy manifested around us.

❖ Our Soul is intended to guide our lives.

❖ Our Soul has a mission, and it incarnates to complete that mission. Each of us can come to know what our Soul mission is.

❖ We are both one with Source energy and seemingly separate at the same time.

❖ Our lives have meaning and purpose.

❖ There are no 'mistakes,' only loving lessons to be learned.

❖ The human being is an energy system, and we can learn to regulate our energy.

❖ Spiritual guidance is continually being offered; we need only to open up and receive it.

❖ We can evolve through joy or suffering. The choice is ours.

❖ It is our inherent right to experience balance and harmony.

❖ The Living in Alignment process empowers us to move out of 'victim consciousness.'

❖ All of life is interconnected and interdependent.

❖ We are our own experts in regard to knowing what is required to experience both personal and Soul fulfillment.

❖ Every circumstance, event, and experience has the 'inherent potential' of providing maximum benefit.

For a complete list, see *Experience Living in Alignment*, Chapter 1: page 8.

T HERE *is no need to struggle to be free; the absence of struggle is in itself freedom.*
Chogyam Trungpa

Chapter 8

Becoming
Internally Resourced

BECOMING internally resourced is a *choice* you make. It's your option to decide whether or not you want to *deepen* your connection with Source energy, *how much* you want to deepen your awareness, and *how conscious* of this connection you want to be.

Developing your capacity to be Living in Alignment is *simple* both in theory and in practice.

Everyone on Planet Earth is already Living in Alignment to a lesser or greater extent, whether or not you are aware of this reality and believe this proposition to be true. Many people are in the dark about their capacity to *accelerate* their process of personal transformation and become increasingly conscious of the *benefits* of Living in Alignment in their daily lives.

Your subjective experiences of Living in Alignment will offer your mind the *proof* it needs to feel confident that Living in Alignment is a practical, effective, and trustworthy approach to living your life, and one that will yield remarkable results.

These subjective experiences of Living in Alignment will also reveal that your Soul is more *capable*, more *qualified*, more *experienced*, and more *skilled* at being in the driver's seat and leading your life than the alternative of relying primarily on the resources of your intellect/mind. This is because our societal conditioning is **limited** by the dominant cultural biases, mores, values, beliefs, perspectives, attitudes, and the like.

T**HE** *beliefs we hold are*
the guardians of our self-image
and our identity.
Richard Barrett

As your mind acknowledges that becoming internally resourced yields *favorable* results — such as

❖ experiencing greater success in your endeavors

❖ feeling confident

❖ developing high self-esteem

❖ having more energy

❖ becoming proficient at manifesting

❖ accessing your Soul mission

❖ developing satisfying relationships

❖ feeling secure in your body and in living your life

❖ experiencing more joy, happiness, and 'freedom to be'

— you will endeavor to be **more conscious** of becoming internally resourced.

Becoming internally resourced is facilitated by attending to *your intuition* (what feels 'right') and learning to listen to and follow the guidance and promptings of your Soul.

Our lack of a healthy connection to our Soul has deluded us into believing that *we are* our ego-centered minds. We think that we are *only* our human selves, that Source energy doesn't exist, that we are *alone* in the Universe, and that life has *no meaning* and purpose. This is the result of being identified primarily with our humanness and being externally resourced. This state of being is referred to as '*mistaken identity*.' Our mental, emotional, physical, and spiritual '*dis*-ease' and conditions are the result of our lack of a healthy connection with our Soul.

Becoming internally resourced is a lifelong practice of *deepening* your connection with Source energy while becoming increasingly aware of the *wondrous unfolding* of your life. From the LIA perspective, Living in Alignment is your *birthright*, a naturally occurring process that is uniquely special to every person.

Your Soul witnesses your human self going about completing your Soul mission, and when you're off-track or heading in that direction, when you need a depth charge, or when certain tasks are coming to completion, your Soul will get the attention of your human self by issuing *wake-up calls* that become more pronounced if not listened to or not followed.

From the perspective of Living in Alignment, you have *free will* regarding the *kind* of relationship you want to have with your Soul, and can *decide* whether or not you want to have a conscious relationship with your Soul.

Becoming internally resourced is much more than having an intellectual understanding of a concept. It is *an alternative way of being and living your life*. It involves changing your orientation *from* being identified primarily with your human self and the *conditioning* of the three-dimensional world *to* having a *conscious connection* with your Soul and *allowing* your Soul to lead your life.

A LL *experiences in the human condition are designed by the soul to serve the purpose of reaching unity consciousness.*
Richard Barrett

There is a *qualitative difference* between being externally resourced versus being internally resourced. The Living in Alignment process will illuminate this difference and assist you to experience it.

Learning to trust the guidance from your Soul is less about figuring out your life and more about *feeling your way* into it. It's not that you stop using your mind or discard logical, rational, linear ways of thinking, but rather that you *apply* these important skills in service of your Soul's directives.

You have the option of *allowing* your Soul to lead your life. The existential answers you seek about the particulars of your life are to be found in the depths of your Soul, *not* within the confines of societal conditioning/dictates. Your life has a unique flow, and you can learn to *trust* and live fully in that flow.

From the Living in Alignment perspective, leading your life from your Soul's directives (versus your mind) is the most desirable, advantageous, and gratifying way to live your life. The more your mind allows your Soul to be in the proverbial driver's seat, the more you will become aware of the wonders of its workings in your life as you gain an increasing assurance of the '*rightness*' of living in partnership with your Soul.

The more internally resourced you become, the more *self-empowered* you become, and the more you move into a position of becoming your own authority.

Your Soul will provide opportunities to place you where you need to be, meeting the people you need to meet, and doing what you need to be doing in each chapter of your life.

Some of the workings of your Soul manifest in all aspects of living your life: synchronicities, dreams, premonitions, revelations, realizations, movies, music, books, through other people, the Ah-ha's, ideas, gut responses. Anything and anybody can serve as a means by which your Soul communicates with you.

A profound *awakening* will occur as you learn to become internally resourced by deferring to your Soul for guidance and following that guidance. The experience of *Soul realization* (the recognition that you have a Soul) leads to *Soul actualization* (living up to your full potential and realizing your Soul mission), which culminates in experiencing *Soul fulfillment*.

Q UANTUM *physics has amply confirmed that matter may be understood as very dense energy. The body may be perceived and understood as energy rather than matter.*
Daniel J. Benor MD and Ruth Benor RN

Chapter 9

'What do you mean by Source energy?'

SOURCE energy is synonymous with *consciousness itself*, which quantum physics has verified as being energy, the wellspring of life, what everybody and everything is made of. This energy is the matrix of life, and it cannot be created or destroyed. It can only be transformed! It is where our zest for living our lives originates. You can become increasingly more aware of how you are *regulating* your energy and *co-creating* your reality.

IF *we are to fully understand our three-dimensional reality, we need to explore the energy field of the fourth dimension of consciousness.*
Richard Barrett

From the perspective of Living in Alignment, Source energy is *a benevolent, intelligent, interactive, creative, ingenious, omnipresent, unifying, self-generating* energy system.

❖ *Benevolent:* Source energy is a loving presence in our lives.

❖ *Intelligent:* Source energy is the wellspring of universal wisdom.

❖ *Interactive:* you can interrelate with Source energy energetically as well as physically in your relationships with all life forms (because you and all life forms are unique reflections of Source energy).

❖ *Ingenious:* Source energy is highly skillful in its ability first to get the attention of, and then to work with your human self/egoic mind.

❖ *Creative:* Source energy is the life force energy inside you that you use to co-create.

❖ *Omnipresent:* Source energy is within all that is.

❖ *Unifying:* Source energy illuminates your interconnectedness with all life forms.

❖ *Self-generating energy system:* Source energy is continuously unfolding, creating, evolving, and transforming.

In addition, Source energy is not static, but in a constant state of evolution.

Although our human minds will never be able to fully comprehend Source energy, you can become increasingly *aware* of the workings of Source energy in your life and in the lives of others. This increased awareness leads to increased understanding.

IT *is not the body
that has an energy field,
but the energy field
that has a physical body.*
Richard Barrett

I am aware that many people have walked away from religious organizations or want **nothing** to do with them. There are many reasons people make the decision to leave religious organizations or choose non-affiliation.

Some of the most common reasons are:

❖ fear of becoming (or feeling they have been) **brainwashed**

❖ not believing the **dogma** these organizations espouse or impose

❖ disagreeing with the **stances** these organizations take

❖ the apparent **hypocrisy**

❖ the **lies**, deceit, and misconceptions perpetuated by religious organizations

❖ the **wars** that have been waged in the name of God and the subsequent **atrocities**

❖ what appears to be **misguided** leadership

❖ the **sexual abuse** endemic within religious organizations

❖ the **misuse** and abuse of power and authority

❖ the psychological, emotional, and spiritual **abuse** that leaders of organizations have inflicted upon people

❖ the inability to respond effectively to the **spiritual** needs of their congregants

From the Living in Alignment perspective, the reasons for people walking away (or running away, as the case may be) from religious organizations are *valid*, *justified*, and at times a *necessary step* to heal and prevent any further assaults on their sensibilities. Behind these reasons for leaving are a trail of unresolved emotional, psychological, and spiritual issues and *impairment*.

❖ Many people who experienced early wounding at the hands of their major caregivers (parents, religious leaders, educators) may transpose these experiences of *neglect*, *abandonment*, and *betrayal* onto a higher Power and thus want nothing to do with it.

❖ Many people who grew up with no concept of a higher Power may consider themselves *atheists* (who don't believe in the existence of a God) or *agnostics* (who claim neither faith in nor disbelief in God and who believe that nothing is known or can be known of the existence or nature of God or of anything beyond material phenomena).

❖ For varied reasons many people have limiting *beliefs*, *perceptions*, and *attitudes* about Source energy, along with unrealistic *understandings*, *expectations*, and *misconceptions*.

❖ In addition, many people have *conflicting* thoughts about, are *angry* with, or hold *resentments* toward Source energy.

❖ Many people live their lives attempting to *pull away from*, *sever*, or *disown* their connection with Source energy and thus *deny* their spirituality.

❖ For some people, their disconnection from Source energy and their spirituality has resulted in living in '*victim consciousness*' or living in quiet desperation.

❖ Others have totally identified with their human condition and are in complete *denial* of the existence (let alone the importance) of their *spiritual nature*. They rely totally on their intellect and are primarily externally resourced. Their belief system is embedded in scientific reasoning: the credo that if something can't be verified scientifically, it doesn't exist.

❖ Other people who feel disconnected from Source energy live *totally in their heads*, having only a peripheral connection with their physical bodies and *missing out* on the experience of being fully human.

❖ Others give the impression that they're *lost souls*.

Many people who have disowned their spirituality often deny, minimize, or are out of touch with how their *unresolved issues* with Source energy are affecting their lives.

Many people think of spirituality as *synonymous* with religion, and because of this have inadvertently and unknowingly attempted to disconnect from their spirituality because *they don't want anything to do with religion*. In other words, many people have mistakenly associated developing their connection with Source energy as being synonymous with religion.

Many people have thrown out the baby with the bathwater when it comes to their spirituality. From the Living in Alignment perspective this is a crying shame! Our *spirituality* is what connects our human self with the deepest core aspect of who we are: our Soul.

Our spirituality is an integral and essential aspect of who we are. By attempting to deny or disown the existence and/or the significance of our spirituality, we are cutting ourselves off from Source energy — our life force!

Ignoring, denying, minimizing, or downplaying the significance of your spirituality are ways in which you *abandon* yourself, creating *discord* between your human self and your Soul that results in a lack of meaning and purpose in your life.

There can be no life (or no life worth living) without being conscious of your vital connection to Source energy.

The Living in Alignment body of work taps into the core of all religious experience, which is the promise of a deepening connection with Source energy, one that *endures* any and all hardship, condition, circumstance, and the like. Living in Alignment is *inclusive* of all religious experiences that endeavor to foster *unity consciousness*.

THE *world view of physics,*
the insights of parapsychology,
and the purview of mysticism
are essentially the same:
a universe of purposeful mind
ever evolving its creation
toward higher consciousness.
Roland Gammon

The Living in Alignment body of work will assist you to move out of *tribal consciousness* (where following a leader is the norm) and experience a direct and *personal connection* with Source energy via your relationship with your Soul.

Living in Alignment fosters an *interdependent* relationship with Source energy as an alternative to either depending on religious leaders to administer to your spiritual needs or disowning your innate spirituality. Your Soul *needs* your human self to be its hands and feet (or its agent), while your human self *needs* your Soul to gain access to the 'bigger picture' of your life.

What if it is true that *all* your circumstances, conditions, events, issues, problems, and concerns are *benefitting* you? And what if it is true that Source energy is *evolving* through each of us via the experiences life offers us? While embracing *all* of your life experiences, you can become increasingly conscious of their significance and the workings of Source energy in your life.

59

Your Soul is a unique manifestation of Source energy. It *lives* simultaneously in both the seen and the unseen worlds. It comes into any particular incarnation with a particular Soul mission. *It does not die* with the death of your physical body.

Your Soul has direct access to the particulars of your life, including *why* you're here and *what* you're here to accomplish and complete within any given lifetime.

IT *is not our level of prosperity*
that makes for happiness
but the kinship of heart to heart
and the way we look at the world.

Both attitudes lie within our power, so that
a man is happy so long as he chooses
to be happy, and no one can stop him.
Alexander Solzhenitsyn

Chapter 10

The Process of Living in Alignment

THE Living in Alignment process will assist you to become increasingly aware of the workings of Source energy in your daily life.

By fostering a partnership with your Soul and letting your Soul be your reference point (to which your mind defers), *the Living in Alignment process will change your life* in remarkable ways.

Your practice of living in partnership with your Soul has a *synergistic effect* on your brain functioning by deepening the dialogue between left and right hemispheres, producing and releasing the chemicals of emotion (endorphins, neurotransmitters, and peptides). This experience happens when you *connect with Source energy* and allow it to *flow freely* throughout your mind and body, rebalancing your brain chemistry and producing an overall sense of health and wellbeing.

The Living in Alignment process will assist you to become increasingly *aware* of and *open* to the *interplay* between your human self and Source energy, feel more *connected* with your humanity, and become more *engaged* in your life.

The Living in Alignment process will hold a metaphoric mirror up to your face, allowing you to see *all* of who you are and *why* you're here. This natural occurrence will highlight the importance of the experiences you're *intended* to have in this lifetime and *each step* you take on your personal journey of transformation.

T**HE** *circumstances of this lifetime are part of the natural flow of an experiential learning system designed by your soul to promote its own evolution.*
Richard Barrett

The Living in Alignment process will illuminate every aspect of your life and be a favorable influence.

The Living in Alignment process will ensure that *both your human and Soul needs get met*, so that you begin to *thrive* in your life instead of merely surviving. From the perspective of Living in Alignment, thriving does not truly occur until your human self is living in *partnership* with your Soul. Instead of viewing your physical life as unimportant, the LIA perspective fosters the viewpoint that your physicality and your life experiences are directly *impacting the evolution* of individual, collective, and universal consciousness.

The Living in Alignment process will assist you to accept fully and *appreciate your humanity* and that of others. This translates to being *receptive and sensitive* to yourself and others as you become consciously present and participate fully in your life experiences.

The Living in Alignment process will open both your mind and heart to the reality that you can serve as a *catalyst* for others and *share* Planet Earth with all interdependent forms of life.

The Living in Alignment process will assist you to *reclaim your spirituality* by providing a working understanding and skill base to develop a partnership with your Soul. Your partnership will facilitate transformative life experiences that are grounded in both the seen and the unseen worlds.

The Living in Alignment process is *pragmatic and experiential*, focusing on assisting you to

❖ have direct *experiences* of the concepts presented

❖ develop *awareness* skills to track your experiences of Living in Alignment

❖ identify the *benefits* being offered

❖ *integrate* these insights, gifts, and lessons into your thinking and behavior.

The Living in Alignment process will assist you to *experience* the qualitative difference between being internally resourced and being externally resourced. As your human self recognizes and acknowledges that being internally resourced is more advantageous and gratifying than being externally resourced, you will feel increasingly more assured that your Soul is *intended* to be in the proverbial driver's seat.

This state of assurance **transforms fear into a knowing** that you can have a personal relationship with Source energy that is primary, dependable, invaluable, and grounded in your physical reality.

T*HE first peace…*
comes within the souls of people
when they realize their relationship,
their oneness with the universe
and all its powers,
and when they realize
at the center of the universe
dwells the Great Spirit,
and that its center
is really everywhere,
it is in each of us.
Nicholas Black Elk

Chapter 11

Benefits of Living in Alignment

HERE are some of the *benefits* that Living in Alignment can offer you:

❖ become your own best friend and ally

❖ gain the skill base to form nurturing relationships

❖ allow other people to be catalysts for you

❖ become self-empowered

❖ live more in your body

❖ develop a partnership between your human self and your Soul

❖ attain a knowing that you are deeply loved

❖ experience heightened creativity

❖ experience a sense of abundance

❖ find inner joy

❖ discover Soul realization, Soul actualization, and Soul fulfillment

❖ gain skills to deal effectively with stress and reduce anxiety

❖ develop more honest and satisfying relationships

❖ create balance and harmony in your life

❖ experience an abiding sense of peace and serenity

❖ discover meaning and purpose in your life

❖ experience freedom to be and fulfill your Soul mission

❖ develop a newfound respect, honor, and appreciation for your human self and your Soul

❖ embody an attitude of gratitude and celebration of life

❖ experience inspired living

❖ gain a renewed sense of belonging

❖ recognize and acknowledge the significance of your life

❖ experience increased spontaneity, fun, and enjoyment

❖ acquire more confidence and a sense of security

❖ make a difference/contribution in the world

❖ expand your mind

❖ become more present

❖ open your heart to yourself, others, and to living your life

❖ connect with your Soul mission

❖ experience sustainable transformation

❖ thrive in your life

For a complete list, see *Experience Living in Alignment*, Chapter 1: pages 14-15.

As soon as you open your mind and heart and begin to align your human self with your Soul, you will experience the benefits of Living in Alignment.

Listening to and following the guidance/promptings from your Soul will always have favorable results — with no exceptions.

The Living in Alignment body of work will help you understand that we are *energy beings* and teach you the skills to *regulate* your energy, live in *balance*, experience *harmony*, and have *blissful* experiences or 'natural highs.'

The Living in Alignment body of work will assist you to develop a *personal philosophy* that is congruent with the way Source energy works in the Universe.

The following are universal principles that govern our lives:

❖ the *attraction* principle (what we think about is what we bring about)

❖ the *polarity* principle (there are many options along a spectrum of possibilities)

❖ the *cause and effect* principle (what goes around comes around)

❖ the *sentience* principle (every belief and perception—and how we process information—is forming or impacting our moment-to-moment experiencing)

❖ the *change* principle (everything is energy and is in a constant state of motion)

❖ the *rhythm* principle (all of life exists within an order, a flow, or a pattern)

❖ the *gender* principle (everything has both masculine and feminine elements)

❖ the *correspondence* principle (the outside world becomes a mirror that reflects how we are experiencing our inner world)

Your direct experiences of the workings of Source energy in your life will reveal that your Soul is more qualified, more adept, more proficient, more skilled, and more experienced to direct your life than your human self (or your mind) when it's *stuck* in the proverbial driver's seat.

WHAT *the spiritual path offers*
is a way to come back into balance,
to develop our intuition
and the wisdom of our heart,
so that the intellect is no longer the master,
but instead is the servant of the heart —
the part of us that brings us into unity
with ourselves and all other beings.
Ram Dass

Chapter 12
The LIA Skill Base

THE Living in Alignment body of work provides a skill base customized to address your needs, concerns, challenges, issues, and the like. Here are some of the skills you'll learn as you integrate the LIA material into your life:

❖ learn to examine the *circumstances* of your life symbolically

❖ increase your capacity to become more present/ aware in your moment-to-moment *experiencing*

❖ identify and take down your mental *defenses*

❖ develop your *intuition*

❖ identify and *integrate* your insights, gifts, and lessons

❖ *open* your heart to yourself and others

❖ develop *healthy* self-esteem

❖ become emotionally *present*

❖ become *your* own best friend/ally

❖ develop functional *boundaries*

❖ *identify* and meet your needs

❖ develop your capacity to live in *balance* and harmony

❖ transform fear- and shame-based realities

❖ open to and become receptive to *change*

❖ become skilled at *focusing*/directing your attention

❖ become adept at *manifesting*

❖ learn to *reframe* the events in your life

❖ develop the skills to avoid getting caught up in the '*drama*' of your own or other people's stories

❖ identify, modify, change, or replace your *limiting* beliefs

❖ individuate and differentiate (to become your own *person*)

❖ work effectively with your *abandonment* issues

❖ identify underlying *causes* of your distress, emotional pain, predicaments, challenges, issues, etc.

❖ expand your *mind*

❖ learn to come to *your own* rescue

❖ improve your ability to *regulate* your energy

❖ develop your capacity to give and receive *love*

I*N the last resort we must begin to love in order that we may not fall ill.*
Sigmund Freud

Chapter 13

Living in Alignment and Relationships

LIVING in Alignment fosters experiencing deeper and more satisfying connections within all of your relationships.

Trust and Surrender are distinct features of your capacity to be intimate. From the perspective of Living in Alignment, the most effective way to develop intimacy with yourself and in all your relationships is by increasing your ability to Trust in and Surrender to your Soul.

Your ability to be loving in all of your relationships is directly proportional to the degree to which your heart is open to yourself. Likewise, being your own best friend and ally is reflected in your ability to demonstrate these qualities in your relationships with others.

IT *is only through relationships that we find truth and meaning in our lives and encounter ourselves.*
Richard Barrett

By embracing your humanity you will come to understand that you're *not perfect*, which translates to making '*mistakes*'. From the perspective of Living in Alignment, these so-called 'mistakes' are viewed as important learning opportunities or '*gifts*' in your development.

Forgiving yourself as well as others is another important ability to develop. The act of forgiveness prevents or frees you from resentments and facilitates emotional intimacy.

The Living in Alignment approach will reveal how your mind is getting in the way or *preventing intimacy* in your relationships.

The Living in Alignment process will assist you to *identify* expectations, attitudes, limiting beliefs, mental defenses, perceptions, unresolved issues, wounding, fears, shame, and dysfunctional behaviors that are preventing you from living authentically and experiencing 'freedom to be'.

Developing intimacy in your relationships is contingent upon seeing and being seen. This translates to showing up for your life and being present and accounted for.

Your own *shaming messages* keep you enslaved to the prejudices of others. The way in which you relate to and treat yourself will be reflected in how other people treat you. You will come to realize that not only do you experience wounding in your relationships, you usually have a need to experience healing there as well.

Your ability to connect with your Soul and to love your human self is the key to experiencing a *deepening* in all your relationships.

N*O snowflake ever falls in the wrong place.*
Zen proverb

The state of your *internal* reality is *reflected* back to you in the quality and depth of your interactions in your relationships in the external world.

For example, feeling alone and fearful are indicators that your human self is *disconnected* from your Soul or Source energy. The less connected you are to your Soul, the more alone you feel and the more fearful you become.

People are *intended to be catalysts* for one another: to serve one another.

In relationships that enhance individual growth:

❖ you shine the light of *truth* upon peoples' attributes, strengths, shortcomings, and talents

❖ you help people to recognize their *life themes*

❖ you serve as a *guide* and team player to accomplish goals and as a *messenger* to let people know when they're off track

73

❖ you assist people to identify and *integrate* their insights, gifts, and lessons.

When you embody the concept that we are all *interconnected* and *interdependent*, you will come to know how to truly be *of service* to others.

It is crucial to establish and maintain a *healthy relationship* with your human self as well as with your Soul. If you identify exclusively with either one, you will create *imbalances* in your life.

You will discover that as you seek to experience a deeper connection with yourself, Source energy, and the people in your life, *attending to* both your human needs and your Soul needs becomes a necessity.

If your personal philosophy is not based on what is true in the Universe, you will create a life that will keep you enmeshed in your humanness and in the human condition, and stuck in '*victim consciousness*' to a lesser or greater extent.

Having inadequate or inappropriate *coping skills* to manage life on its terms manifests as:

❖ not being emotionally *present*

❖ being afraid of *intimacy*

❖ not being able to *identify* or meet your needs

❖ being highly *defended*

❖ an inability to be *spontaneous*

❖ feeling *victimized*

- being *needy*/dependent
- having *low* self-esteem
- *isolating* behaviors
- having *poor* social skills
- emotional *immaturity*

PEACE *of mind comes not from wanting to change others, but by simply accepting them as they are.*
Gerald G. Jampolsky

The LIA body of work emphasizes developing your relational skills as well as learning to *accept* living your life on its terms. If you have not developed adequate processing skills, you will tend to *project* your unresolved issues onto others.

Shame is what keeps a person living in 'victim consciousness.' Unconscious shame will manifest in many different forms of *self-abandonment:*

- *not* taking care of your basic human needs
- living in *deprivation*
- *internalized* anger
- *submissiveness*
- *rage*

❖ being *careless*

❖ being *irresponsible*

❖ *negative* self-talk

❖ other self-abusive and *self-sabotaging* behaviors

When you live in 'victim consciousness' you will be forever entangled in your *'story'* or caught up in the *'drama'* happening in your life or the lives of others. As a result you will tend to *abuse* yourself and/or allow others to abuse you.

Your Soul knows what the *'right'* relationship is with all of the people in your life and will inform your human self. In this context, 'right' refers to how you can best *enhance* each other's growth and personal transformation.

The Living in Alignment process will assist you in examining your **behaviors, cognitions,** and **beliefs** about relationships to determine whether or not they facilitate or *prevent* you from experiencing deeper connections.

Expect and *normalize* that whatever **gets *in the way*** of your deepening relationship with your Soul will present itself in your relationship with your human self and with others. This is revealed in ways that get your mind's attention — another reason to attend to your lived experience.

Deepening with your Soul involves assisting your human self to *get out of your way*. This is done in a loving manner!

OTHERS *are merely mirrors of you.*
You cannot love or hate something
about another person unless it reflects
something you love or hate about yourself.
Anonymous

The Living in Alignment process is designed to highlight whatever *gets in the way* of your functioning effectively in relationships, such as:

❖ *unresolved* issues

❖ *unrealistic* expectations

❖ *addictions*

❖ *limiting* beliefs

❖ *maladaptive* behavioral patterns/coping skills

❖ *resentments*

❖ *fears*

❖ *shame*

❖ *guilt*

❖ *anger*

Some simple measures to keep your heart open to yourself and others are to stop

❖ *judging,*

❖ *shaming,*

❖ *fault-finding,*

❖ *guilt tripping,* and

❖ *blaming* yourself or others.

IN *today's highly interdependent world,*
individuals and nations
can no longer resolve
many of their problems
by themselves.

We need one another.

We must therefore develop
a sense of individual responsibility....

It is our collective and
individual responsibility
to protect and nurture
the global family,
to support its weaker members,
and to preserve and tend
the environment in which we live.
The Dalai Lama

Chapter 14

Living in Alignment and Living in Community

ON both the individual and collective levels a *deepening* of awareness is taking place on Planet Earth. A *critical mass* (or tipping point) has been reached whereby a significant number of people now *tune inwardly* to receive their guidance. This phenomenon indicates that humans are *evolving* from five sensory beings to six sensory beings by tuning in and developing their intuition.

The Living in Alignment Model was developed to meet a growing need and demand from people interested in *accelerating* their personal transformation. The primary focus of the model is to offer people a working understanding and skill base to discover a relationship with Source energy by fostering a *partnership* between their human self and their Soul.

The Living in Alignment process of becoming internally resourced assists people to develop their capacity to become increasingly more aware of the *workings* of Source energy in their lives and in the lives of others.

Among the many benefits of connecting with your Soul and Living in Alignment is *discovering your Soul mission*.

From the perspective of Living in Alignment, *everyone* has a Soul mission! It is your *birthright* and destiny to discover your Soul mission and to accomplish it.

Discovering your Soul mission will illuminate the *significance* of your life. As more and more people make a choice to go inward to connect with their Soul and access their Soul mission, they will experience a newfound *freedom*. Knowing your Soul mission is self-empowering, for it gives your life a *profound sense of meaning and purpose*.

The Living in Alignment process moves people out of 'victim consciousness' by revealing the *significance* of all the circumstances, positions, and situations that have happened or are happening in their lives.

Here is a list of *insights* and *qualities* that are generated and fostered as you deepen your connection with your Soul and begin Living in Alignment:

❖ all of life is interconnected and *interdependent*

❖ be a *unifying* presence

❖ be of *service* to others

❖ *celebrate* diversity

❖ become *solution-focused*

❖ become *proactive*

❖ develop a *transformational* presence

❖ view yourself as an *exemplar*

- ❖ develop an '*us*' mentality
- ❖ focus on doing the '*right*' thing
- ❖ lead from your *Soul*, not from your egoic mind
- ❖ develop an attitude of *gratitude*
- ❖ avoid '*drama*'
- ❖ *transcend* dualism
- ❖ open up to *possibilities*
- ❖ *trust* and surrender to Source energy

T**HE** *real, the great period of human fulfillment on planet earth is only now about to begin.*
Robert Muller

Becoming internally resourced is self-empowering. When you connect with your Soul, you access your *authentic self*. By listening to and following your Soul's guidance, you are able to live authentically.

When you are self-empowered, you become *self-motivated*. You no longer wait for so-called leaders to lead, for you see yourself as a leader in your own right, as well as everyone else. In your daily living this translates to becoming *proactive* about doing what you're being called to do in the lives of others and in your own life.

When you acknowledge that you are interconnected and interdependent with all life forms, your mind opens to the importance of being a *catalyst* for others and the necessity of becoming a *steward* of Planet Earth and all life forms.

As you discover that becoming internally resourced is always *advantageous* and a practical, effective, and trustworthy *alternative* for living your life, you will endeavor to listen to and follow the guidance from your Soul.

The Living in Alignment process illuminates the insights, gifts, and lessons *being offered* in your life experiences. As you integrate this information in your mind, it will facilitate *internal shifts* that will be reflected externally, having a *transformative* effect on your functioning in all aspects of your life.

W E *are members
of a vast cosmic Orchestra
in which each living instrument
is essential to the complementary
and harmonious playing
of the Whole.*
J. Allen Boone

As you become internally resourced, you will move naturally from a '*me*' mentality to an '*us*' mentality. This translates to becoming more conscious of your *impact* on others and vice versa, along with becoming more *service-oriented*. A life of service takes many and varied forms.

You may be called to *affiliate* with various organizations to be a *neutralizing* influence or work to bring about *transformative change* within a particular system.

You may be drawn to initiate a *grassroots* cause or movement.

You may be called to be a parent of a special needs child, to be a Red Cross nurse or doctor, to live a monastic life, to be a shaman, or to be a politician, etc. The possibilities of a life of service are *limitless*.

In the Living in Alignment Program, groups come together to support, inspire, heal, celebrate, and *empower* participants. They also come together for fellowship, to share life experiences, identify solutions, and create a safe environment to practice and *integrate* their Living in Alignment skills.

As you access and deepen in your practice of becoming internally resourced and Living in Alignment, you will become more *assured* that your Soul will *guide* you where you need to go, meeting the people you need to meet, and doing what you need to be doing.

Being a *catalyst* for other people and *allowing* people to be catalysts for you is yet another way that your becoming internally resourced and Living in Alignment will influence people around you. This phenomenon highlights how we are interconnected and *interdependent* upon one another. Being catalysts also offers us a renewed sense of *trust* in ourselves and in others.

As diverse as these roles can be in a life of service, they all share one thing in common: assisting you to live up to your full potential and fostering *unity consciousness* across Planet Earth.

When you are living in unity consciousness, you are naturally inclined to identify the *needs* of your community and work with people 'in the know' to do what it takes to come together and provide for these needs.

To say that becoming internally resourced and Living in Alignment fosters unity consciousness is an understatement, for Living in Alignment is *all* about unity consciousness. When you begin to grasp this truth, you will find yourself opening your mind and heart to the 'bigger picture' of the human condition and understand that you are here to be of *service* to others.

As you practice Living in Alignment, you will become an *exemplar* of going within and developing a relationship with Source energy.

T**HE** *human race is in the midst of making an evolutionary leap. Whether or not we succeed in that leap is* your *personal responsibility.*
Scott Peck

Chapter 15

Experience Living in Alignment
A Practical Guide to Personal Transformation

EXPERIENCE *Living in Alignment* serves as a comprehensive resource for people who are interested in applying the Living in Alignment approach to their lives and for those who are participating in the Living in Alignment Program.

The information presented in the Living in Alignment body of work is a synthesis of universal principles/wisdom that has been distilled from many masters and from many traditions. This information is essential for your human self to partner with your Soul as you begin Living in Alignment.

Experience Living in Alignment will provide you with a working understanding and skill base to open your mind and heart to the reality that developing a partnership between your human self and your Soul is your natural state of being. The areas of focus have proven effective in ensuring that your human self/mind is successful in aligning with your Soul. The information is presented in clear, concise, and simple terms.

This knowledge and skill base is intended to both accelerate and ground your personal process of transformation.

Experience Living in Alignment emphasizes having direct experiences of the Core Concepts, along with identifying and integrating the insights, gifts, and lessons you are learning in the Living in Alignment process.

Experience Living in Alignment consists of twelve chapters and seven appendices, along with a glossary of terms and a reading list. The author's personal story introduces each chapter, followed by the main text, a list of main points, and integrative activities designed to give you the opportunity to have direct experiences of the subject matter. The seven appendices identify and address practical considerations, issues, and challenges that will arise as you engage in the Living in Alignment process.

Here are synopses of the information found in each of the chapters and appendices:

Chapter 1
Living In Alignment With Your Soul:
An Overview

Offers a clear understanding of the LIA Model. With the author's personal introduction, the Program Objectives, the Core Concepts of the LIA Model, a chart comparing the perspectives of your Ego vs. your Soul, the Benefits of Living in Alignment, the '*Is Living in Alignment For You?*' self-test, and the poem *This Longing*.

Chapter 2
Opening Your Heart

Describes what it means to open your heart, and how your capacity to love others is proportional to your capacity to love yourself. Opening your heart is the gateway to your Soul, and the starting point for experiencing and understanding the process of Living in Alignment.

Chapter 3
What is Source Energy?

Invites you to examine your beliefs about a higher Power to illuminate how they impact every aspect of your life. Presents concepts that have proven effective in expanding self-awareness and deepening your relationship with Source energy. Understands Source energy as a living reality.

Chapter 4
Your Essential Spirituality

Explores distinctions between religion and spirituality and your reality as a spiritual being. Emphasizes embracing your individuality, developing a spiritual practice, finding meaning and purpose, experiencing self-empowerment, and meeting the needs of both your human self and your Soul.

Chapter 5
Forming Healthy Relationships

Illuminates the concept that you are both human and divine. Explores the impact of societal conditioning on individual wellbeing. Introduces the value of acting as catalysts for one another and moving out of victim consciousness. Offers best practices in relationship skills.

Chapter 6
Examining Your Beliefs and Cognitions

Highlights the function of your beliefs and cognitions in co-creating your reality. Explores your experiential knowing versus the beliefs systems that influence us. Offers skills for modifying, changing, or replacing beliefs and cognitions that limit your mind's access to your Soul.

Chapter 7
Resolving Power and Authority Issues

Focuses on specific attributes of power and their significance in your life. Discusses your tendencies to give away your power and how to resolve issues around power and authority. Examines the abuse of power in positions of leadership. Offers skills for reclaiming your power.

Chapter 8
Developing Your Awareness

Proposes that self-awareness is a skill that each of us can learn. Addresses how self-awareness can alter your unconscious conditioning and why it can be difficult. Suggest that conscious living is a personal choice, and that increased self-awareness is key to becoming internally resourced.

Chapter 9
Working with Universal Energy

Advocates the premise that we are energy beings in a universe of energy. Offers universal principles that govern how energy works in your life, Presents a clear understanding of how to use these principles to focus your energy and facilitate your ability to manifest your Soul's directives.

Chapter 10
Opening to Transformation

Highlights transformation as the natural, ongoing process of deepening self-awareness that affects all aspects of your life. Explores living with impermanence, change, and life stages in the context of the cycle of life, death, and rebirth. Introduces the challenge of sustaining transformation in your life.

Chapter 11
Learning to Trust and Surrender

Affirms that Trust and Surrender are experiential states of being, accessible with practice, and an approach to living your life. Offers that Trust and Surrender are integral to embodying your Truth and deepening your connecting with your human self, others, and Source energy.

Chapter 12
The Process of Living in Alignment

Deepens your grasp of the Living in Alignment Process, identifies experiences, cognitions, and feelings that may be elicited, while normalizing and utilizing them for transformation. Shows how to discern your Soul's voice, utilize resistance, work with dark forces, and optimize Living in Alignment with your Soul.

Appendix A
Skills for practicing Living in Alignment

An extensive list of the skills to practice with each module of the Living in Alignment Program to help you increase your awareness, become internally resourced, and deepen your experience of Living in Alignment.

Appendix B
What to Keep in Mind when Experiencing Fear

A list of transformative methods for being with and working with fear. When you are externally resourced, your focus is primarily on survival, not the needs of your Soul, and you do not have access to the 'bigger picture' view of your life.

Appendix C
Protocol for Being in a
Waiting or Gestation Period

Practices for dealing with the uncertainty of being in a waiting period. Includes developing trust, managing your emotions, maintaining a contemplative presence, deepening your relationship with your Soul, and deferring to your Soul's journey.

Appendix D
Protocol for Connecting with, Listening to, and Following the Promptings of Your Soul

Offers methods to quiet the mind, develop your ability to distinguish your Soul's voice, and follow your Soul's guidance. Includes deprogramming your mind from limiting beliefs and cognitions and recognizing your Soul's messages.

Appendix E
Protocol for Staying Present

Practices proven to help you to stay present to your moment-to-moment experiencing. Focusing your attention and intention on staying present will increase your awareness. Your human self is intended to be a clear channel for your Soul as well as to serve as its hands and feet.

Appendix F
What Are Energy 'Blocks' and Energy 'Leaks'?

Practices that help you recognize how your life may be compromised by energy 'blocks' and energy 'leaks', monitor your energy flow, energize your human self, reclaim your vitality, maintain balance and harmony, and live an empowered life.

Appendix G
Ego-Centered Consciousness vs.
Living in Alignment

Describes how your ego-centered consciousness is disconnected from awareness of your Soul/Mystery. Explores the ego-centered illusion of duality and the insight that you are both human and divine.

T**HERE** *is no greater victory in the life of a human being than victory over the mind.*
Swami Ramdas

Chapter 16

Glossary

Clarification of Terms used in
the Living in Alignment Model

A **DDICTION:** Something you *have*, not who you are. As with all conditions (mental, emotional, physical) if viewed from your Soul's perspective, addictions can be utilized for the purpose of transformation. Addiction is a strategy your human self chooses to try to control (cope with) life challenges.

Authenticity: Fully accepting yourself as both human and divine. It is knowing that the best gift you can offer is to genuinely be real with yourself and others in all of your relations. Being authentic is about living your truth, which is how you become and stay empowered. Your authenticity serves as an invitation for others to be authentic.

B **OUNDARIES:** Limits you place on yourself and others. They are to be established and maintained as a means to: (1) protect yourself from others; (2) protect others from yourself; and (3) protect yourself from harmful conduct or thinking.

C **ONDITIONS:** The mental, emotional, physical, sexual, or spiritual energy patterns everyone has. (Nevertheless they are not *who* we are.) Conditions have the 'inherent potential' of serving to facilitate your awareness and the unfoldment of

Source energy. How you relate to them will determine whether or not they keep you hostage or hasten your process of transformation (Soul realization, Soul actualization, Soul fulfillment).

Consciousness: Source energy, a higher Power, God, Buddha, Nature, the Divine, and all other names used to refer to the underlying essence of all things seen and unseen. To have a conscious living experience refers to being aware that we are all manifestations of consciousness itself.

DIVINE: Your expanded consciousness of the spiritual dimension of your life that transcends your human desires; your connection to the mysterious power at the core of your existence that has a transformative influence on your life and destiny.

EGO: A product of your conditioning, this aspect of your mind perceives itself as separate and is primarily preoccupied with your human needs and wants: survival and the pursuit of pleasure. If unchecked, this propensity develops into self-centeredness and narcissism. Once your human self comes sufficiently into Living in Alignment with your Soul, however, it begins to experience more security and love, thereby becoming more willing and able to listen to and follow your Soul's promptings.

Emotion: The energy of different frequencies, in motion, flowing through you. Your Soul communicates to you through the language of emotions. Your emotions offer you valuable information about what is happening in both your internal and external realities.

Emotional Presence: The quality of being able to identify, feel, and appropriately share your feelings with yourself and others.

Energy: The essence of what everyone and everything is made up of. Everything and everyone vibrates at different frequencies of energy. You can learn how to 'partner' with Source energy and become conscious of how it is that you are co-creating your realities with your thoughts, perceptions, behaviors, expectations, beliefs, attitudes, and intentions. Energy is the matrix of consciousness.

Energy 'Block': Energy that gets stuck due to the restriction or constriction of Source energy. You may be aware that 'something' is blocking you from moving forward in your life with clarity and purpose, but you may not have a clue about what you are habitually feeling and/or doing that is creating or perpetuating your 'blocked' energy.

Energy 'Leak': An experience of Source energy (vitality) that is being psychologically and emotionally dissipated to a greater or lesser extent on an ongoing basis. As with energy 'blocks', you may be aware that your energy level is down, but may not have a clue as to what is causing this depletion.

Externally resourced: When you allow outside influences to rule you. This plays out in all aspects of our lives, including the professions we choose, if and whom we marry, how and where we worship, where we live, what make of car we drive, whom we associate with, etc. When you are externally resourced, you will live in fear because your connection to Source energy is minimal and/or not integrated.

FORGIVENESS: The act of releasing someone (or yourself) from a 'mistake' or wrongdoing. Forgiving does not mean forgetting what happened but rather making the choice to let go of resentment and preoccupation with transgressions. Identifying and integrating the insights being offered are effective methods of helping your mind release its grip.

GROUNDEDNESS: Having a secure, felt sense of being in touch with all aspects of your reality (thoughts, emotions, sensations, experiences). Living in your physical body, taking care of your earthly responsibilities, and being fully present in the moment.

HIGHER POWER: Referred to as the Source of everything that is, was, and will be. A benevolent, interactive, ingenious, creative, and unifying energy system, this higher Power is in a constant state of evolution as well as beyond our mental comprehension.

Humanness: Includes your physical body, intellect, and personality.

INTEGRATION: Living your 'knowing' in daily life, 'walking your talk,' living your truth, mind/body unification with your Soul. Integration is the embodiment of your journey from head to heart.

Internally resourced: When you take outside influences into account, but primarily tune in to your inner self to access and in turn follow the directives of your Soul.

L IVING IN ALIGNMENT: The process by which you (as identified with your human self/ personality) come to connect with and attune to your Soul. When this happens, you await and follow its directives, which ensures that your Soul will complete its mission. More specifically, you (your human self) accept your rightful position as the executor of your Soul.

R ECOVERY: In the context of the Living in Alignment Model, recovery refers to the process of reclaiming your personal power (or Source energy) you have given away to addictions, to people, to conditions, to events, and/or to limiting conditioning.

Religion: Refers to individual beliefs and opinions concerning the existence, nature, and/or worship of a deity or deities. The operative word here is 'belief', as opposed to 'knowing' from direct experience. Oftentimes those who are 'religious' think that they need an intermediary to connect with a higher Power. In addition, those who are 'religious' tend to give their power away to outside authority and/or get caught up in dogma.

S EEN REALITY: Refers to the three-dimensional world that is perceived by our five senses.

Shame: A feeling that results from thinking 'I am bad' or 'something is wrong with me; I am not OK; I am not lovable; I am not enough,' etc. It is a combination of dishonor, unworthiness, and embarrassment. Shame is not something you are born with; it is the result of your earthly conditioning (of not being 'seen' and treated as a spiritual/sacred being).

Shame-based reality: When you choose to become identified with your shame, you experience yourself as inferior (which gets played out as operating in a one-up or one-down position with others), as well as seeing yourself and your life as worthless. A shame-based reality is the result of: (1) not being fully acknowledged as a unique reflection of Source energy; (2) being taught that you are a sinner and that your life is about repenting; (3) having experienced traumatic events and interpreting these events from a place of blaming and holding yourself responsible; (4) years of self-deprecation; (5) living with people who are shaming.

Soul: Who you are in your deepest nature. Your Soul is your essence. Each Soul is a unique aspect and reflection of Source energy. It continues to exist after the body dies.

Soul actualization: Living up to your greatest potential as well as realizing your Soul mission in the physical world.

Soul fulfillment: Your experience of deep and abiding peace, joy, and happiness as you manifest your Soul mission.

Soul mission: What your Soul yearns to realize in this world: your freedom to be fully human, to manifest your unique potential, and to engage with passion the particular circumstances you have co-created with Source energy.

Soul realization: Occurs when you both recognize and acknowledge that on the deepest level of your being, you are a living, breathing aspect of Source energy (which is referred to as your Soul) manifested in a physical body. It is knowing that all life forms are manifestations of Source energy, that 'We are all ONE.' In addition, it is knowing that your presence in a physical body living on Planet Earth is important and that your life has meaning and purpose.

Source energy: A benevolent, interactive, ingenious, creative, omnipresent, unifying, and self-generating energy system, Source energy is in a constant state of evolution as well as beyond your mental comprehension. It is the wellspring of everything that is, was, and shall be.

Spiritual awakening: Developing your intuitive awareness that: (1) as a spiritual being in a physical body, you are both human and divine; (2) you are a unique reflection of, and have direct access to Source energy; (3) the unseen is as real as what you see; (4) all life forms are sacred, interconnected, and interdependent; (5) your life has meaning and purpose and is important in the evolution of consciousness.

Spiritual bypassing: Avoiding certain aspects of your earthly existence by focusing on spiritual beliefs and practices at the expense of denying the importance of your earthly experiences. This can take the form of 'meditating' away your uncomfortable feelings, living in denial, minimizing aspects of your reality, not taking responsibility for your life, not holding yourself accountable for your decisions and choices, not taking care of your basic needs and/or expecting others or Source energy to do it for you, leading your life from a place of entitlement, etc.

Synchronicity: An energetic phenomenon (a seeming coincidence) that occurs when you are asking for and aligning with the greatest potential of what wants to happen in any given moment or situation. You can view it as a confirmation that something of importance is occurring. This may take many forms, such as a person coming into your life at a crucial time; a new opportunity; a solution to a problem, etc.

'Story', The: The rigid ideas you construct around the events you experience (past and present). When you are stuck in your story, you become fixated on the literal interpretation of what is happening in your life (what you make out to be the facts). In other words, you may find yourself getting stuck in your cognitions. Subsequently, drama ensues in terms of who is to blame and who is right; resentments build, nothing gets resolved, and you stay focused on your problem.

Sustainable Transformation: A lifelong process of integrating insights, gifts, and lessons from your Soul's interaction with your human self that sustains an internal shift in your awareness: focusing on the Soul mission you are intended to have and enabling you to accomplish it in the context of your life circumstances while also meeting your human needs.

UNITY CONSCIOUSNESS: Your embodied experience of connecting with Source energy or consciousness itself, being at One with all creation, and transcending polarizing perspectives (right /wrong, good/evil, sexual/spiritual, mind/body, self/ other, human/divine).

Unseen Reality: The world beyond three-dimensional reality. That which you cannot perceive with your five senses but can experience through your intuition.

YOUR *vision will become clear*
only when you look into your heart.
Who looks outside, dreams.
Who looks inside, awakens.
Carl Jung

HUMAN *being is part of...the Universe*
— a part limited in time and space.
He experiences himself,
his thoughts, and feelings
as something separated from the rest —
a kind of optical delusion
of his consciousness.

This delusion is a kind of prison for us,
restricting us to our personal desires
and to affection for a few persons nearest us.

Our task must be to free ourselves
from this prison
by widening our circle of compassion
to embrace all living creatures
and the whole of nature in its beauty.

Nobody is able to achieve this completely,
but the striving for such achievement
is in itself a part of the liberation
and a foundation for inner security.
Albert Einstein

Chapter 17

Integrative Activities

YOU are encouraged to try the following Integrative Activities to deepen your felt sense of Living in Alignment in your life. Each chapter of *Experience Living in Alignment* includes additional Integrative Activities.

Opening Your Heart

1) A In a comfortable sitting or lying down position, place one hand on top of the other over your heart. Begin breathing normally, in and out through your nose or through your mouth, whichever way feels right to you. Now begin to breathe in one quality of an ***open heart*** (unconditional love, understanding, forgiveness, kindness, generosity, compassion, etc.), simply breathing in this quality, and breathing out this quality. Do this for a couple of minutes (10-15 breaths). All the while pay attention to what you are ***experiencing*** as you're breathing in and breathing out.

B Afterwards, speak to yourself out loud about what you're experiencing in the moment, or if you prefer, write it down or draw an image.

2) A In a comfortable position, begin to focus on taking in a slightly deeper breath at a normal pace, and when you breathe out make sure all the air is expelled before you take another breath in. As you are breathing in and out, visualize what it would look like to be *your own best friend* and ally, and to come to your own rescue. Do this for a few minutes, paying attention to any *thoughts* or *feelings* that are surfacing.

B Afterwards, spend some time tuning in to what you are thinking and feeling, noticing any changes in your energy level, mood.

3) A In a comfortable position, begin to focus on taking in a slightly deeper breath at a normal pace, and when you breathe out make sure all the air is expelled before you take another breath in. As you are breathing in and out, visualize looking at yourself and *forgiving yourself* for some behavior (past or present) that you have shame or guilt about. Do this for a few minutes, paying attention to any thoughts or feelings that are surfacing.

B Afterwards, spend some time tuning in to what you are thinking and feeling, noticing any changes in your energy level, mood.

To explore opening your heart, see *Experience Living in Alignment*, Chapter 2: Opening Your Heart.

What is Source Energy?

1) A Visualize and breathe into the *image* you have of Source energy (or a higher Power).

B What *thoughts* and *feelings* are surfacing about your relationship with Source energy?

2) A Imagine that Source energy is sitting in a chair in front of you.

B Express your *thoughts* and *feelings* to Source energy.

C What is this experience like? What *insights* about your relationship with Source energy did you access?

To explore Source energy, see *Experience Living in Alignment*, Chapter 3: What Is Source Energy?

Your Essential Spirituality

1) A Write the word 'SPIRITUALITY' in the center of a blank piece of paper and, while repeating it to yourself, write whatever words, statements, or symbols that come to mind (write nonstop for 3 minutes).

B Afterwards, look over everything you wrote down while tuning in to any insights or impressions.

C Describe your experience of this exercise.

2) A On a piece of paper (or notebook) make two columns, one for *Spirituality* and one for *Religion*. Write down the distinctions between the two in short, concise statements.

B Compare the lists and notice what thoughts and/or feelings are surfacing.

C What did you learn or find out?

To explore your spirituality, see *Experience Living in Alignment*, Chapter 4: Your Essential Spirituality.

Forming Healthy Relationships

1) A Identify what you have an aversion to or difficulty *accepting* in other people.

B Identify what you have an aversion to or difficulty accepting in *yourself*. (Keep in mind that 'acceptance' doesn't mean you have to *like* a behavior, character trait, or particular physical attribute, but it does translate to not avoiding, denying, or minimizing your personal reality).

C Experience what happens in your relationship with self and others as you begin to *accept* what you have an aversion to in yourself.

2) A Practice making *eye contact* with people when you are engaging with them.

B Tune in to what this experience is like. What do you notice in your body? What *feelings* or *thoughts* arise? How does this affect your interactions?

3) A Identify *unfinished business* (a concern, issue, problem) you have within one of your relationships.

B Determine which course of action to take to *resolve* the matter and become proactive in doing so (you may require some professional assistance with this).

C Afterwards, describe the mental, emotional, and physical *differences* you experience.

To explore your relationships, see *Experience Living in Alignment*, **Chapter 5: Forming Healthy Relationships.**

Examining Your Beliefs and Cognitions

1) A Write about a belief, perception, or attitude that you have since *modified* or changed.

B How did it *change* you or your life?

2) A Make a list of the *beliefs*, *perceptions*, or *attitudes* you have about yourself.

B Place a check mark next to or highlight the ones that you think are *getting in your way*.

C How would you *modify*, *change*, or *replace* that belief, perception, or attitude?

To explore your beliefs and cognitions, see *Experience Living in Alignment*, Chapter 6: Examining Your Beliefs and Cognitions.

Resolving Power and Authority Issues

1) A For 3 minutes write nonstop about whatever comes to mind when you repeat the statement 'When I think about becoming *self-empowered*, what surfaces is…'

B Read what you have written down.

C What draws your attention and why?

2) A Write the word '**POWER**' in the center of a blank piece of paper and, like a mantra, keep repeating it while jotting down whatever words or phrases come to mind.

B Using the word '**AUTHORITY**', repeat this exercise.

C What *insights* do you have about your relationship with these words? How do you think your responses to these words are *impacting* you and your life?

To explore your power and authority issues, see *Experience Living in Alignment*, Chapter 7: Resolving Power and Authority Issues.

Deepening Your Awareness

1) Do you want to become *more aware*? Why or why not?

2) Track your body sensations *before* and *after* making decisions. Doing so will give you confirmation of the 'rightness' of those decisions.

3) A Start becoming *more aware* of your surroundings, thoughts, body sensations, emotions, words, and actions.

B How does becoming more aware *impact* your experiences?

4) Make a list of what you consider to be the *advantages* and *disadvantages* of becoming more aware. Make two columns.

To explore deeper levels of awareness, see *Experience Living in Alignment,* Chapter 8: Deepening Your Awareness.

Partnering With Source Energy

1) A For the next 3 minutes *experience* what occurs when you are putting yourself down (repeat statements that you regularly make).

B What do you feel *emotionally*? What are the *sensations* in your body?

2) A For the next 3 minutes *experience* what occurs when you are saying self-affirming statements to yourself.

B What do you feel *emotionally*? What are the *sensations* in your body?

3) Focus on what you *want* to have happen in your life instead of focusing on what you *don't* want. Take note of the differences in your energy in each case.

To explore partnering with Source energy, see *Experience Living in Alignment*, **Chapter 9: Partnering with Source energy.**

Opening To Transformation

1) A Write nonstop for 3 minutes on what comes to mind when you think about the statement 'When I think about *change*...'

B Read what you wrote. What gets your attention and why? What *insights* can you glean about the *impact* of change upon yourself and/or your life from having done this exercise?

2) A Make a list of the ways in which you *resist* change.

B What *impact* does resisting change have on your life?

3) A What would happen in your relationship to 'change' if you knew that change is *always* for your benefit?

B Instead of resisting the changes that are occurring in you life (or for that matter in the lives of others), start being *receptive* to them. What are you aware of when you do this?

To explore your transformation, see *Experience Living in Alignment*, **Chapter 10: Opening To Transformation.**

Learning To Trust And Surrender

1) A Describe what you have experienced when you *trusted* in and *surrendered* to Source energy by listening to and following the guidance/promptings of your Soul.

B What were the *benefits* of having done so?

2) What has *facilitated* your ability to both Trust and Surrender? What has *impeded* your ability to both Trust and Surrender?

3) How do you *know* when you're trusting Source energy?

To explore Trust and Surrender, see *Experience Living in Alignment*, Chapter 11: Learning to Trust And Surrender.

The Process Of Living In Alignment

1) Identify and list ways in which you *increase* your energy frequency.

2) Do a stream-of-consciousness writing on 'When I think about my *intuition*, what surfaces is...'

3) Visualize the image of a river and think about the fact that your life has a *flow*. As you consider this image, what have you learned about being *in the flow* of your life?

To explore the Living in Alignment process, see *Experience Living in Alignment*, Chapter 12: The Process of Living in Alignment.

Exploring Living in Alignment

HERE are several ways to experience Living in Alignment in your life:

❖ Do the Integrative Activities suggested in Chapter 17, pages 103-109 of this book.

❖ Read *Experience Living in Alignment* and do the Integrative Activities (self-directed).

❖ Organize or attend an LIA Workshop or Presentation offering you the opportunity to experience the Living in Alignment Model. Presentations are designed to meet the specific needs of sponsoring organizations.

❖ Receive individual and or group psychotherapy, addiction recovery counseling, or Life coaching.

❖ Participate in the Living in Alignment Program.

❖ Consult with a certified LIA facilitator.

❖ Train to become a certified LIA facilitator.

Living in Alignment Resources

The Living in Alignment Program will provide a working understanding and skill base to help you partner effectively with your Soul, and offers customized professional facilitation to help you integrate transformative experiences and sustainable practices into your daily life.

Visit the **LivingInAlignment.ca** website for more information, resources, and current events.

Books by Darcy S. Clarke
available from the CreateSpace eStore or Amazon.com

Experience Living in Alignment: A Practical Guide to Personal Transformation. This comprehensive Guide makes a distinct contribution to the process of experiencing personal transformation, providing a universal human roadmap to illuminate, support, and facilitate your personal growth.

Saying 'Yes!' to You and Your Life: Thriving in Recovery: the Living in Alignment Approach offers a broader perspective on the origin and treatment of dependence, placing your sustained recovery in the context of your spiritual journey: discovering and coming home to yourself.

Healing the Wounds of Codependence will assist you to reclaim your life by developing both a working understanding of the sources of your codependent patterns and a practical skill base essential to your personal wellbeing and self-empowerment.

The CreateSpace Edition is Printed in USA   ISBN: 978-0-9917101-6-4